## THIRD SERIES

# New Classics to Moderns

Works by Le Roux, J.S. Bach, Seixas, Haydn, Clementi,
Mozart, Mussorgsky, Tchaikovsky, Chopin, Nielsen, Swinstead,
Stravinsky, Lutoslawski, Bennett, Chapple, Hurd.

# 3

Edited by Sam Lung.
Music processing and layout by Camden Music Services.

Order No. YK22132
ISBN 978-1-78305-370-4

## Yorktown Music Press, Inc.

DISTRIBUTED BY

Visit Hal Leonard Online at
**www.halleonard.com**

World headquarters, contact:
**Hal Leonard**
7777 West Bluemound Road
Milwaukee, WI 53213
Email: info@halleonard.com

In Europe, contact:
**Hal Leonard Europe Limited**
1 Red Place
London, W1K 6PL
Email: info@halleonardeurope.com

In Australia, contact:
**Hal Leonard Australia Pty. Ltd.**
4 Lentara Court
Cheltenham, Victoria, 3192 Australia
Email: info@halleonard.com.au

# Contents

# Passepied

## from Pièces de Clavessin (Suite I)

Gaspard Le Roux
1660–1707

# 2-Part Invention No.10 in G Major

## BWV 781

Johann Sebastian Bach
1685–1750

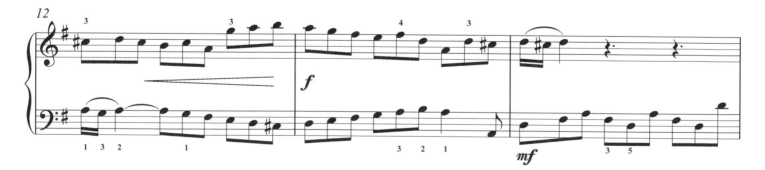

# Musette

Johann Sebastian Bach
1685–1750

**Andante pastorale**

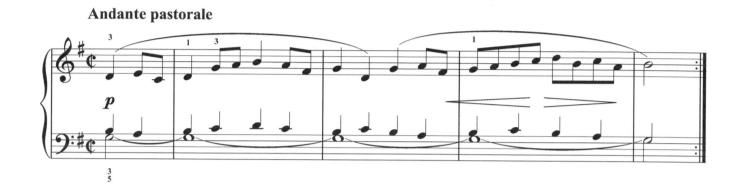

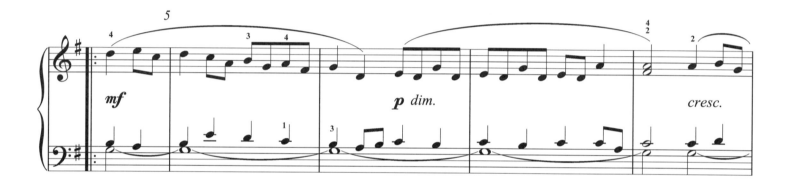

# Giga

*from* Sonata in D Minor

José Carlos de Seixas
1704–1742

# Menuet and Trio

*from* Sonata in A Major, Hob.XVI:5

Joseph Haydn
1732–1809

**MENUET**
**Allegretto** ♩ = 104

**TRIO**

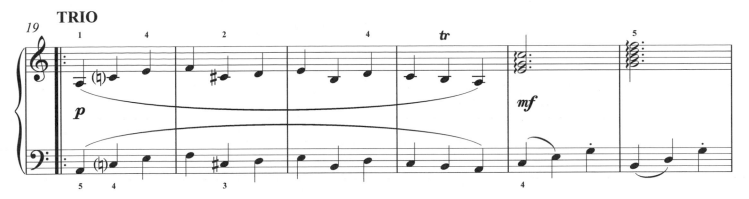

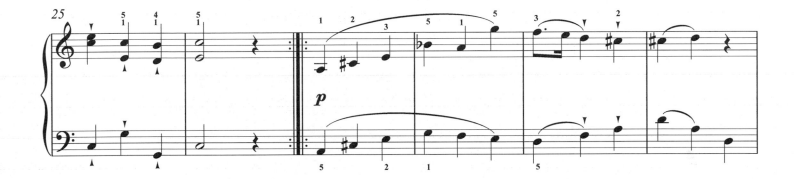

**Menuet da capo al Fine**

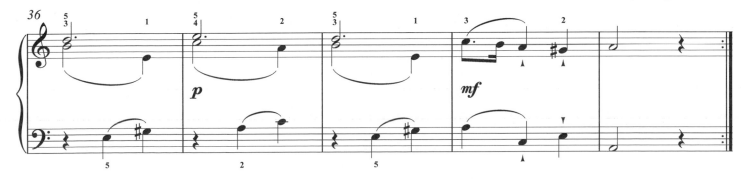

# Sonatina in F Major, Op.36 No.4

## 1st Movement

Muzio Clementi
1752–1832

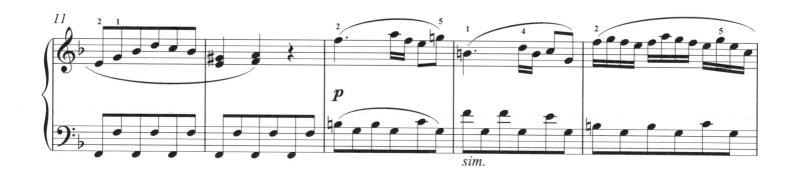

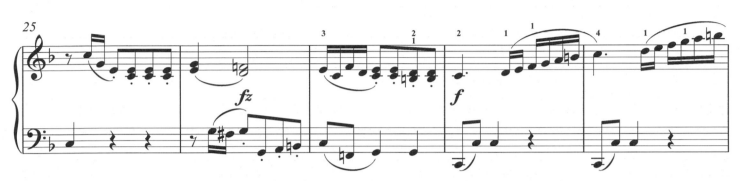

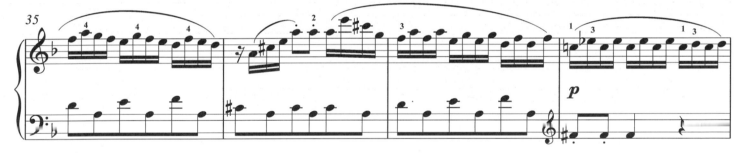

# Rondo, K.15d

No.4 *from* The London Sketchbook

Wolfgang Amadeus Mozart
1756–1791

# Promenade

*from* Pictures At An Exhibition

Modest Mussorgsky
1839–1881

**Allegro giusto, nel modo russico, senza allegrezza, ma poco sostenuto**

# Maman

## *from* Album For The Young

Peter Ilyich Tchaikovsky
1840–1893

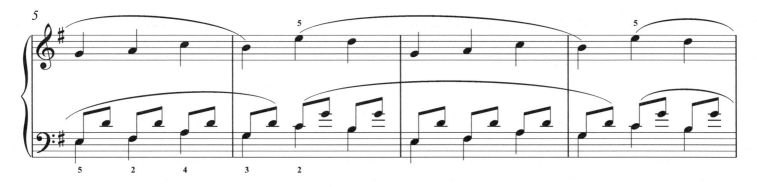

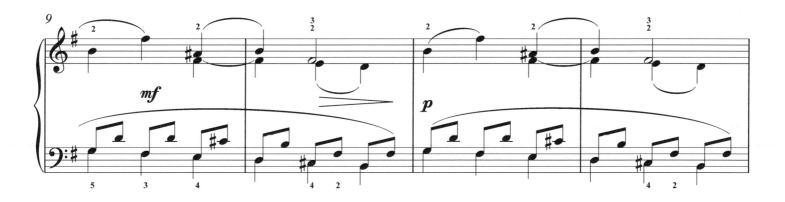

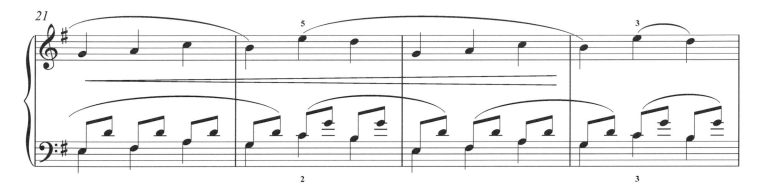

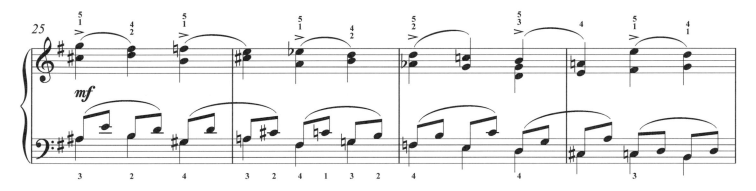

poco ritard.

# Mazurka in F Major, Op.68 No.3

Frédéric Chopin
1810–1849

**Allegretto, ma non troppo**

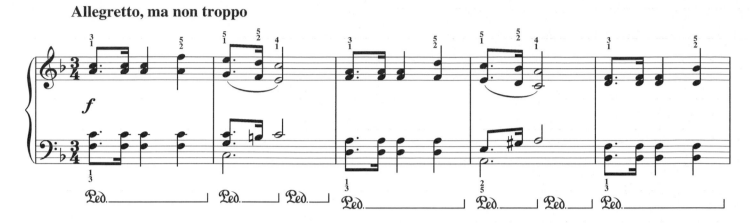

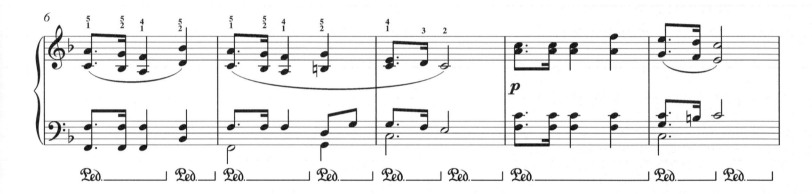

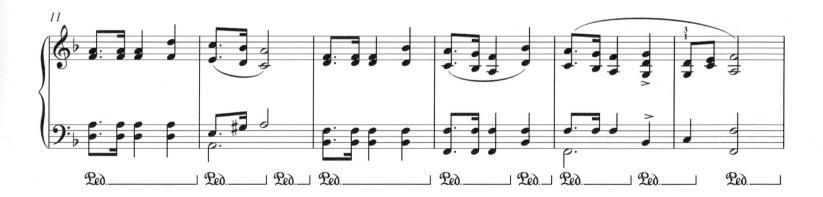

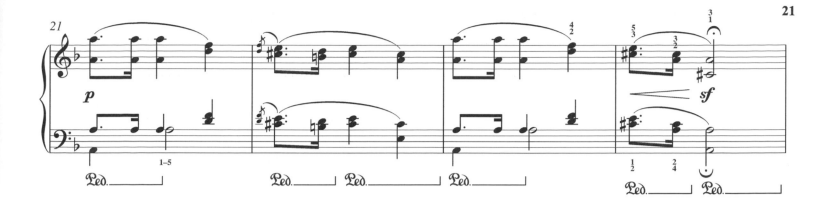

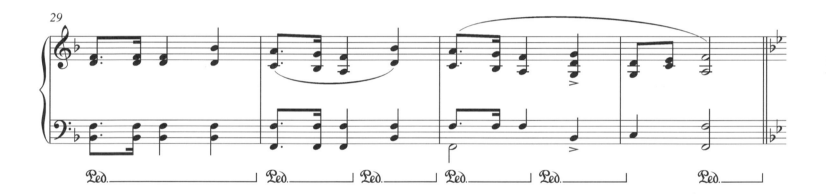

**Poco più vivo**

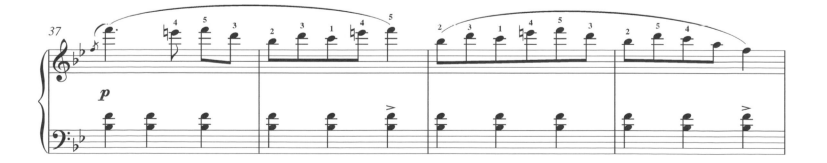

rit.

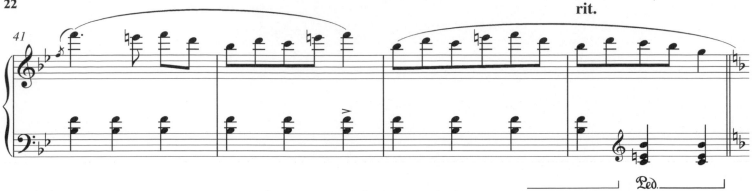

**Tempo I**

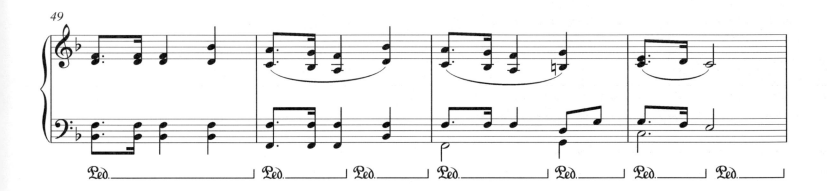

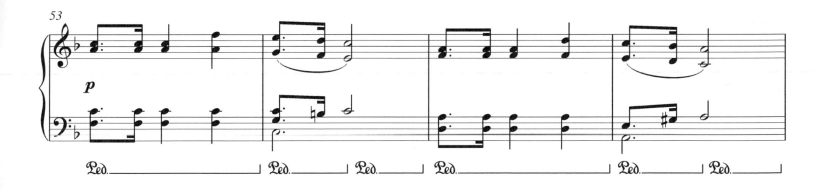

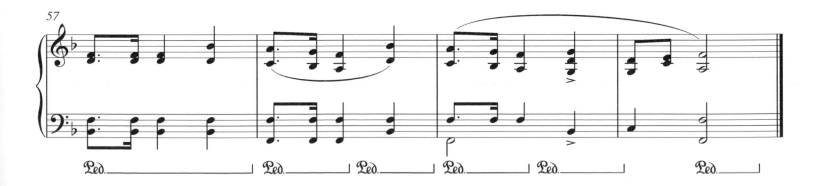

# Piano Music For Young And Old
## No.1

Carl Nielsen
1865–1931

**Allegretto** ($\quarternote$ = *c*.76)

# In Solitude

*from* Five Pastels, Op.51

Felix Swinstead
1880—1959

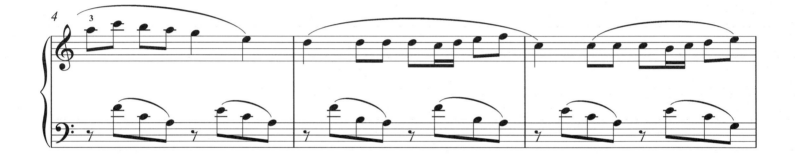

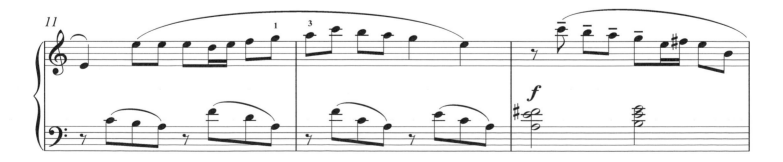

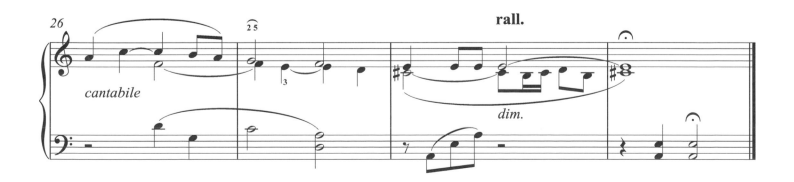

# Allegretto

No.3 *from* Les Cinq Doigts

Igor Stravinsky
1882–1971

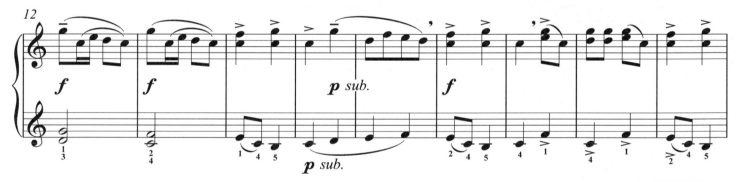

# There Is A Path There Is

*from* Folk Melodies

Witold Lutoslawski
1913—1994

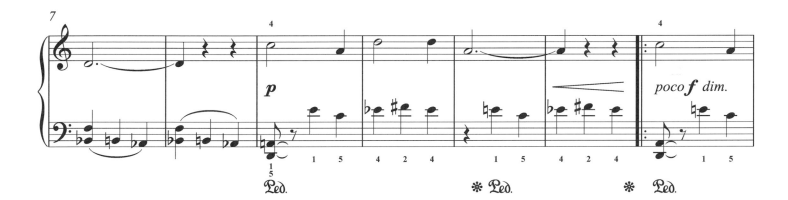

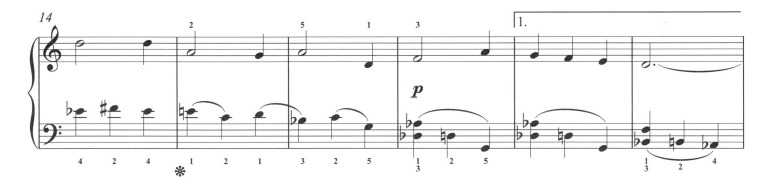

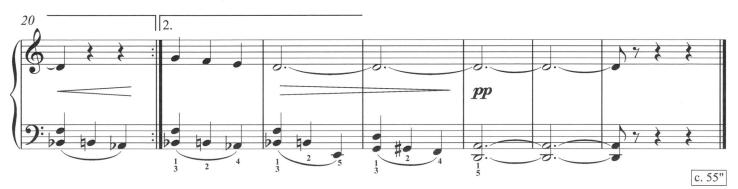

c. 55"

# Little Elegy

Richard Rodney Bennett
1926–2012

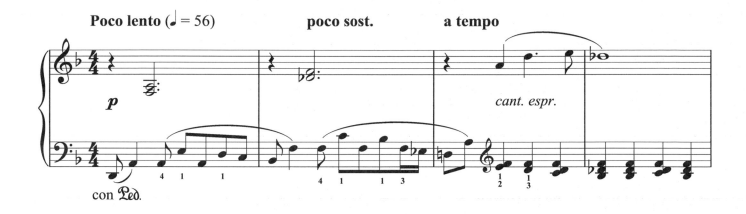

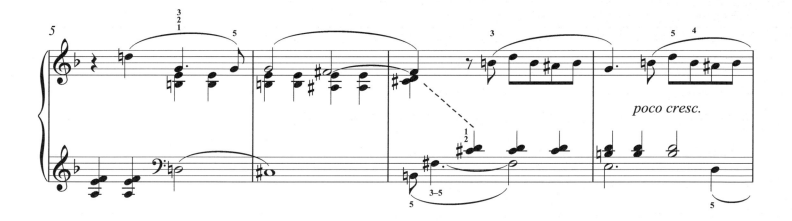

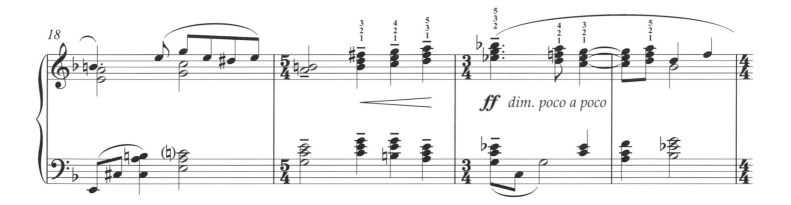

# Far From Home

*from* In The Pink

Brian Chapple
b.1945

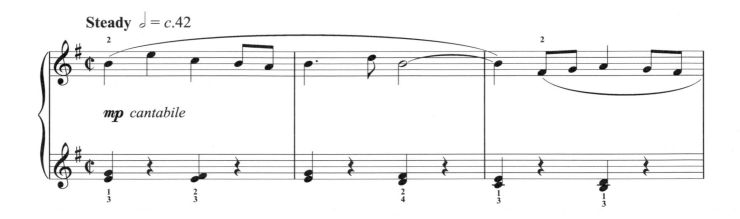

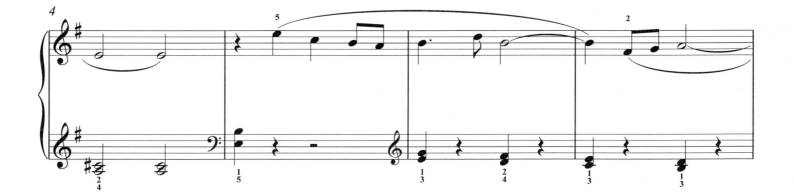

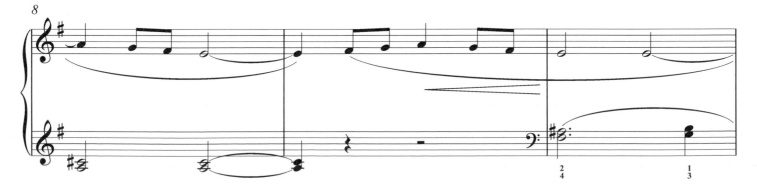

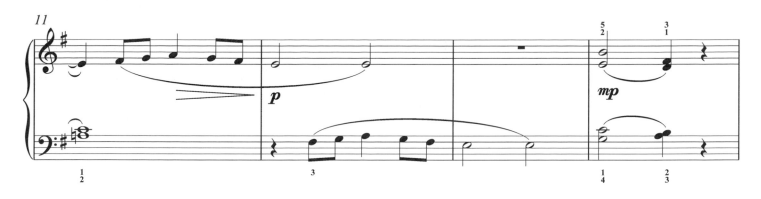

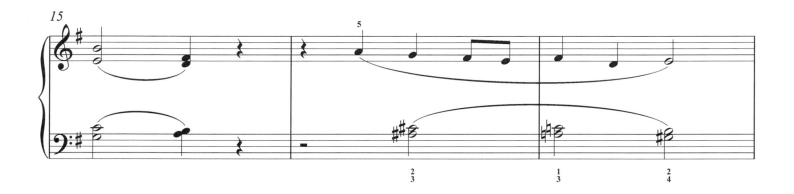

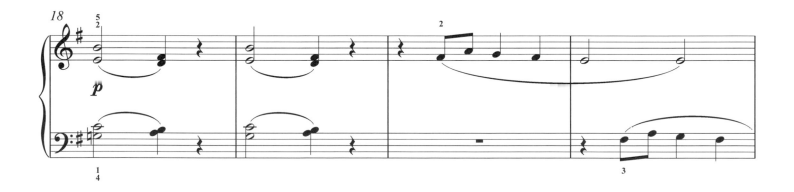

# Contrasts

*from* Bagatelles

Michael Hurd
1928–2006

**Allegro moderato**

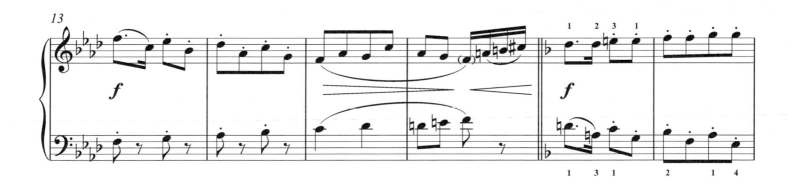

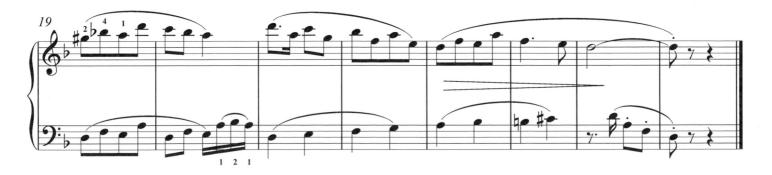